TO ....

FROM ....

CREATE THE HIGHEST, GRANDEST VISION POSSIBLE FOR YOUR LIFE, BECAUSE YOU BECOME WHAT YOU BELIEVE.

OPRAH WINFREY

THERE CAN BE NO GREATER GIFT THAN THAT OF GIVING ONE'S TIME AND ENERGY TO HELP OTHERS WITHOUT EXPECTING ANYTHING IN RETURN.

NELSON MANDELA

You must never be fearful
about what you are
doing when it is right.

ROSA PARKS

WHAT MATTERS IS
NOT WEALTH, OR
STATUS, OR POWER,
OR FAME, BUT
RATHER HOW WELL
WE HAVE LOVED.

Barack Obama

WHAT YOU'RE SUPPOSED
TO DO WHEN YOU DON'T
LIKE A THING IS CHANGE IT.
IF YOU CAN'T CHANGE IT,
CHANGE THE WAY YOU
THINK ABOUT IT.

Maya Angelou

Education is the passport to the future, for tomorrow belongs to those who prepare for it today.

Malcolm X

I FEEL LIKE PEOPLE ARE EXPECTING ME TO FAIL; THEREFORE, I EXPECT MYSELF TO WIN.

LEWIS HAMILTON

I WAS TAUGHT
I HAD BASIC RIGHTS
AS A HUMAN BEING.
I WAS TAUGHT
I WAS SOMEONE.

Sidney Poitier

DON'T EVER MAKE
DECISIONS BASED
ON FEAR. MAKE
DECISIONS BASED ON
HOPE AND POSSIBILITY.
MAKE DECISIONS
BASED ON WHAT
SHOULD HAPPEN, NOT
WHAT SHOULDN'T.

Michelle Obama

I am driven by two main philosophies: know more today about the world than I knew yesterday and lessen the suffering of others. You'd be surprised how far that gets you.

NEIL deGRASSE TYSON

MAN IS A UNIVERSE WITHIN HIMSELF.

BOB MARLEY

LOOK AT PEOPLE FOR AN
EXAMPLE, BUT THEN MAKE
SURE TO DO THINGS YOUR
WAY. SURROUND YOURSELF
WITH POSITIVE PEOPLE.

Queen Latifah

ANYTHING CAN BE ACHIEVED WITH A GOOD, HEALTHY DOSE OF COURAGE.

VIOLA DAVIS

I don't
think limits.

Usain Bolt

IN THE DARK TIMES, IF YOU HAVE SOMETHING TO HOLD ON TO, WHICH IS YOURSELF, YOU'LL SURVIVE.

WHOOPI GOLDBERG

We're all the authors
of our own destiny.
We have to take control
and do our best to
leave our mark
while we're here.

SHEA COULEÉ

LEARN TO SPEAK LIKE
YOUR VOICE DESERVES
TO BE HEARD...
PLACE YOURSELF IN
THE FRONT, RISE UP
AND <u>STAND FIRM IN
WHAT YOU BELIEVE IN.</u>

CHIDERA EGGERUE

YOU WORK HARD,

YOU MAKE YOUR

OWN LUCK.

RIO FERDINAND

You have to be able
to accept failure
to get better.

LeBRON JAMES

I HAVE MY FLAWS,
BUT I EMBRACE
THEM AND I LOVE
THEM BECAUSE
THEY'RE MINE.

Winnie Harlow

JUST DECIDE WHAT IT'S
GONNA BE, WHO YOU'RE
GONNA BE, HOW YOU ARE
GOING TO DO IT... AND FROM
THAT POINT, THE UNIVERSE
WILL GET OUT OF YOUR WAY.

Will Smith

Challenge yourself; it's the only path which leads to growth.

Morgan Freeman

YOUR LIFE IS YOUR STORY, AND THE ADVENTURE AHEAD OF YOU IS THE JOURNEY TO FULFILL YOUR OWN PURPOSE AND POTENTIAL.

KERRY WASHINGTON

BEAUTY IS NOT JUST PHYSICAL. IT'S ABOUT WHAT YOU STAND FOR, HOW YOU LIVE YOUR LIFE.

Halle Berry

DON'T LET SUCCESS GET TO YOUR HEAD OR FAILURE GET TO YOUR HEART.

Anthony Joshua

You are beautiful:
embrace it.
You are intelligent:
embrace it.
You are powerful:
embrace it.

MICHAELA COEL

WHEN YOU WALK UP TO OPPORTUNITY'S DOOR, DON'T KNOCK IT... SMILE AND INTRODUCE YOURSELF.

DWAYNE JOHNSON

THE MIND IS EVERYTHING. IF YOU DON'T BELIEVE YOU CAN DO SOMETHING THEN YOU CAN'T.

Kai Greene

PORTRAY THE WORLD FOR WHAT IT IS AND YOU WILL FIND TRUTH.

JOHN BOYEGA

If everything
was perfect,
you would never
learn and you
would never grow.

Beyoncé

I AM THE SOLE

AUTHOR OF THE

DICTIONARY THAT

DEFINES ME.

ZADIE SMITH

If you have an opportunity to use your voice you should use it.

SAMUEL L. JACKSON

YOU HAVE TO BELIEVE IN YOURSELF WHEN NO ONE ELSE DOES — THAT MAKES YOU A WINNER RIGHT THERE.

VENUS WILLIAMS

A LIFE IS NOT IMPORTANT EXCEPT IN THE IMPACT IT HAS ON OTHER LIVES.

JACKIE ROBINSON

Hard work. Dedication.
Prayers and belief...
That's all it takes.

FLOYD MAYWEATHER JR

MY JOB IS TO NEVER
GET OFF THE ROAD.
I MAY HAVE TO
SWITCH LANES,
BUT I HAVE NEVER,
EVER GOTTEN
OFF THE ROAD.

Stacey Abrams

EVERY GENERATION LEAVES
BEHIND A LEGACY. WHAT
THAT LEGACY WILL BE IS
DETERMINED BY THE PEOPLE
OF THAT GENERATION.

John Lewis

You can't accept someone's opinion, simply because they say they don't think you're good enough.

Ian Wright

ONLY IN DARKNESS CAN YOU SEE THE STARS.

MARTIN LUTHER KING JR

I'M GOING TO SPEAK THE
TRUTH WHEN I'M ASKED
ABOUT IT... THIS ISN'T
FOR PUBLICITY...
THIS IS FOR PEOPLE THAT
DON'T HAVE THE VOICE.

Colin Kaepernick on sitting
for the national anthem

SUCCESS IS NOT
ACHIEVED BY
WINNING ALL
THE TIME.
REAL SUCCESS
COMES WHEN WE
RISE AFTER WE FALL.

Muhammad Ali

It is in your hands
to create a better world
for all who live in it.

NELSON MANDELA

DON'T SETTLE FOR OTHER PEOPLE'S LIMITS. THEY DON'T KNOW YOU. GIVE EVERYTHING YOUR ALL, BECAUSE EVERYTHING BECOMES POSSIBLE ONCE IT'S DONE.

DINA ASHER-SMITH

TRUTH IS POWERFUL, AND IT PREVAILS.

Sojourner Truth

YOU MAY NOT
CONTROL ALL THE
EVENTS THAT
HAPPEN TO YOU,
BUT YOU CAN
DECIDE NOT TO BE
REDUCED BY THEM.

MAYA ANGELOU

My vision for my career is too precious to let loose among the naysayers. Don't feed your dreams to the lions.

Bernardine Evaristo

A TIME WHEN

WE HAVE TO SH

OUR FEAR AND

GIVE HOPE TO

EACH OTHER.

THAT TIME IS N

The only way to discover
the limits of the possible,
is to go beyond them
to the impossible.

GEORGE FOREMAN

JUST ABOUT ANYBODY
IS A BIG GIRL IN A
SMALL WORLD BUT
YOU GOTTA BELIEVE IT
ON THE INSIDE, THAT
YOU CAN BE BIGGER
THAN THE REST OF IT.

LIZZO

TRUTH IS A LETTER FROM COURAGE!

ZORA NEALE HURSTON

IT'S OKAY IF
YOUR PERSONAL
DEFINITION IS
IN A CONSTANT
STATE OF FLUX
AS YOU NAVIGATE
THE WORLD.

JANET MOCK

IN COMPLETE
DARKNESS WE ARE
ALL THE SAME.
IT IS ONLY OUR
KNOWLEDGE AND
WISDOM THAT
SEPARATES US.
DON'T LET YOUR
EYES DECEIVE YOU.

Janet Jackson

A LOVE OF BOOKS HAS OPENED
SO MANY DOORS FOR ME.
STORIES HAVE INSPIRED ME
AND TAUGHT ME TO ASPIRE.

Malorie Blackman

Not everything
that is faced
can be changed.
But nothing can
be changed until
it is faced.

James A. Baldwin

OUR UNITY IS OUR STRENGTH, AND OUR DIVERSITY IS OUR POWER.

KAMALA HARRIS

I DON'T NEED TO
BE VALIDATED BY
ANYBODY ELSE,
I DON'T NEED TO
BE ACCEPTED OR
APPROVED OF FOR
MY HAPPINESS.

Letitia Wright

REAL FEARLESS AND
FIERCE WOMEN
COMPLEMENT OTHER
WOMEN AND WE
RECOGNIZE AND
EMBRACE THAT THEIR
SHINE... ACTUALLY
MAKES OUR LIGHT
SHINE BRIGHTER.

Gabrielle Union

Go get yours.
Go conquer the world.

STORMZY

WE'RE ALL CAPABLE OF CLIMBING SO MUCH HIGHER THAN WE USUALLY PERMIT OURSELVES TO SUPPOSE.

OCTAVIA E. BUTLER

DON'T BE AFRAID TO
THINK OUTSIDE THE BOX.
DON'T BE AFRAID TO FAIL
BIG, TO DREAM BIG.

Denzel Washington

STORIES HAVE BEEN USED TO DISPOSSESS AND TO MALIGN. BUT STORIES CAN ALSO BE USED TO EMPOWER... STORIES CAN ALSO REPAIR THAT BROKEN DIGNITY.

CHIMAMANDA NGOZI ADICHIE

Differences in experience, points of view and opinions aren't what pulls us apart. It's what pulls us together.

Tracee Ellis Ross

ONCE YOU FI

YOUR VOICE,

AND YOU'RE

CONFIDENT,

YOU SHOULD

TAKE THAT AN

RUN WITH IT.

We're born with success. It is only others who point out our failures, and what they attribute to us as failure.

WHOOPI GOLDBERG

WHEN YOU CAN'T
FIND SOMEONE
TO FOLLOW,
YOU HAVE TO FIND
A WAY TO LEAD
BY EXAMPLE.

ROXANE GAY

IF I CAN CREATE

THE MINIMUM

OF MY PLANS

AND DESIRES

THERE SHALL BE

NO REGRETS.

BESSIE COLEMAN

Life is so much bigger, grander, higher, and wider than we allow ourselves to think.

QUEEN LATIFAH

WE CAN'T
PLAN LIFE.
ALL WE CAN
DO IS BE
AVAILABLE
FOR IT.

Lauryn Hill

NEVER SAY NEVER,
BECAUSE LIMITS,
LIKE FEARS,
ARE OFTEN JUST
AN ILLUSION.

Michael Jordan

Survival isn't lying down and saying, "Oh, poor me." It's finding ways to live and keep your light shining in the midst of the darkest circumstances.

Danai Gurira

IF YOU HAVE
SOMETHING TO SAY
OF ANY WORTH
THEN PEOPLE WILL
LISTEN TO YOU.

OSCAR PETERSON

BREAK A VASE, AND THE LOVE
THAT REASSEMBLES THE
FRAGMENTS IS STRONGER
THAN THAT LOVE WHICH TOOK
ITS SYMMETRY FOR GRANTED
WHEN IT WAS WHOLE.

Derek Walcott

DON'T SIT DOWN
AND WAIT FOR THE
OPPORTUNITIES
TO COME.
GET UP AND
MAKE THEM.

Madam C. J. Walker

Greatness comes from fear. Fear can either shut us down and we go home, or we fight through it.

LIONEL RICHIE

KEEP YOUR EYES ON THE FINISH LINE AND NOT ON THE TURMOIL AROUND YOU.

RIHANNA

BE DRIVEN, BE FOCUSED,
BUT ENJOY EVERY
MOMENT, BECAUSE IT
ONLY HAPPENS ONCE.

Alicia Keys

SECRETS WEIGH HEAVY... YOU WASTE ENERGY AGONIZING WHEN YOU COULD BE LIVING YOUR LIFE AND REALIZING YOUR DREAMS.

NICOLA ADAMS

There is a power
that can raise you
up even from the
lowliest of places.

John Lewis

THE ULTIMATE MEASURE
OF A MAN IS NOT WHERE
HE STANDS IN MOMENTS
OF COMFORT AND
CONVENIENCE, BUT
WHERE HE STANDS AT
TIMES OF CHALLENGE
AND CONTROVERSY.

MARTIN LUTHER KING JR

You have to decide for yourself how you are going to respond, and respond in a way that is not detrimental to your well-being.

ROSE HUDSON-WILKIN

WE NEED TO DO A BETTER JOB PUTTING OURSELVES HIGHER ON OUR OWN "TO DO" LIST.

MICHELLE OBAMA

WE ALL REQUIRE
AND WANT
RESPECT;
MAN OR WOMAN,
BLACK OR WHITE.
IT'S OUR BASIC
HUMAN RIGHT.

ARETHA FRANKLIN

I, too, am America.

LANGSTON HUGHES

IF THERE IS
NO STRUGGLE,
THERE IS
NO PROGRESS.

Frederick Douglass

BESIDE THE NETTLE,
EVER GROWS THE
CURE FOR ITS STING.

Mary Seacole

Tolerance, compassion and consideration are the key to happiness.

Floella Benjamin

WE CAN WORK TOGETHER
FOR A BETTER WORLD
WITH MEN AND WOMEN
OF GOODWILL, THOSE WHO
RADIATE THE INTRINSIC
GOODNESS OF HUMANKIND.

WANGARI MAATHAI

HARD WORK AND TRAINING. THERE'S NO SECRET FORMULA.

Ronnie Coleman
on success

NEVER EVER REFER TO YOURSELF AS "LUCKY" TO BE EXACTLY WHERE YOU'RE MEANT TO BE. YOU WORKED FOR THIS. TAKE THE CREDIT. ABSORB THE PRAISE. DANCE IN THE LIGHT. THIS WAS ALL YOU.

Chidera Eggerue

You can't be
hesitant about
who you are.

VIOLA DAVIS

I believe that
telling our stories,
first to ourselves
and then to one another
and the world,
is a revolutionary act.

JANET MOCK

I BELIEVE EACH INDIVIDUAL CAN HAVE A SAY AND MAKE A DIFFERENCE.

MALORIE BLACKMAN

IF THERE'S A BOOK YOU WANT TO READ, BUT IT HASN'T BEEN WRITTEN YET, THEN YOU MUST WRITE IT.

Toni Morrison

The chances you take, the people you meet, the people you love, the faith that you have. That's what's going to define your life.

Denzel Washington

WHEN I DARE TO BE POWERFUL – TO USE MY STRENGTH IN THE SERVICE OF MY VISION – THEN IT BECOMES LESS AND LESS IMPORTANT WHETHER I AM AFRAID.

AUDRE LORDE

The most important thing, the thing that unites all of us, is that we can inspire and challenge one another to be better.

KOBE BRYANT

THE WAY TO BRING ABOUT CHANGE IS TO BE PROACTIVE AND ACTIVE.

OCTAVIA SPENCER

WITHIN YOURSELF

THERE'S A TALENT,

A GIFT, A PURPOSE

THAT NEEDS TO

BE FULFILLED

AND YOU NEED

TO DO IT.

STORMZY

Sometimes you can do everything right and things will still go wrong. The key is to never stop doing right.

ANGIE THOMAS

KNOWLEDGE
SPEAKS, BUT
WISDOM LISTENS.

Jimi Hendrix

BEAUTY FOR ME MEANS
CONFIDENCE AND COMPLETE
COMFORT IN YOURSELF,
DISREGARDING WHATEVER
ANYONE SAYS TO YOU
OR WHAT SOCIETY SAYS
YOU SHOULD BE.

Philomena Kwao

I like to choose
compassion
over judgement
and curiosity
over fear.

Tracee Ellis Ross

SUCH AS I AM, I AM A PRECIOUS GIFT.

ZORA NEALE HURSTON

WOMEN OF COLOUR COULD BOLDLY SAY TO THE WORLD, "HEY, LOOK AT ME! I'M HERE AND I HAVE VALUE AND I AM BEAUTIFUL."

Beverly Johnson
on being the first Black model to
appear on the cover of *Vogue*

I'LL TELL YOU
WHAT FREEDOM
IS TO ME.
NO FEAR.
I MEAN, REALLY,
NO FEAR!

Nina Simone

Breaking those barriers is worth it. As much as anything else, it is also to create that path for those who will come after us.

KAMALA HARRIS

EXPERIENCE COMES TO US FOR A PURPOSE, AND IF WE FOLLOW THE GUIDANCE OF THE SPIRIT WITHIN US, WE WILL PROBABLY FIND THAT THE PURPOSE IS A GOOD ONE.

RUBY BRIDGES

DON'T DREAM OF WINNING, TRAIN FOR IT.

Mo Farah

THE MOST COMMON WAY PEOPLE GIVE UP THEIR POWER IS BY THINKING THEY DON'T HAVE ANY.

ALICE WALKER

Every moment
is not great and
sometimes those
are the moments
in which you
learn the most.

Allyson Felix

YOU'RE BRILLIANT,
YOU KNOW THAT?
YOU CAN ACHIEVE
ANYTHING
YOU PUT YOUR
MIND TO.

JESSICA ENNIS-HILL

God made me the way
I am and I accept myself.
I am who I am and
I'm proud of myself.

CASTER SEMENYA

YOU'VE GOT TO WANT TO BE THE BEST, EVERY SINGLE DAY.

THIERRY HENRY

CHANGE WILL NOT
COME IF WE WAIT
FOR SOME OTHER
PERSON OR SOME
OTHER TIME...
WE ARE THE
CHANGE THAT
WE SEEK.

BARACK OBAMA

Don't be afraid to be yourself just because you're not like everybody else in class.

RIHANNA

WHAT WE DO
IS MORE
IMPORTANT THAN
WHAT WE SAY OR
WHAT WE SAY
WE BELIEVE.

bell hooks

THE MOST LUXURIOUS
POSSESSION, THE RICHEST
TREASURE ANYBODY HAS, IS HIS
PERSONAL DIGNITY.

Jackie Robinson

Waking up in truth is so much better than living in a lie.

Idris Elba

THE STRUGGLES ALONG THE WAY ARE ONLY MEANT TO SHAPE YOU FOR YOUR PURPOSE.

CHADWICK BOSEMAN

YOU ARE ON THE EVE OF
A COMPLETE VICTORY.
YOU CAN'T GO WRONG.
THE WORLD IS BEHIND YOU.

Josephine Baker

OUTSIDERS OFTEN
HAVE AN INSIGHT
THAT AN INSIDER
DOESN'T QUITE HAVE.

Diane Abbott

Sometimes,
what you're looking for
is already there.

ARETHA FRANKLIN

DON'T EVER STOP.
KEEP GOING.
IF YOU WANT
A TASTE OF
FREEDOM,
KEEP GOING.

HARRIET TUBMAN

I'M NOT GOOD
AT EVERYTHING,
I JUST DO MY BEST
AT EVERYTHING.

Michael B. Jordan

DON'T GO BACKWARDS — YOU'VE ALREADY BEEN THERE.

RAY CHARLES

Caring for myself is not self-indulgence. It is self-preservation, and that is an act of political warfare.

Audre Lorde

THE MORE YOU
PRAISE AND
CELEBRATE
YOUR LIFE,
THE MORE THERE
IS IN LIFE TO
CELEBRATE.

OPRAH WINFREY

The success of every
woman should be the
inspiration to another.
We should raise
each other up.

SERENA WILLIAMS

DON'T COUNT THE DAYS, MAKE THE DAYS COUNT.

MUHAMMAD ALI

THE ONLY WAY IS

TO FIGHT YOUR

WAY OUT AND

KEEP GOING

UNTIL THE DREAM

COMES TRUE.

KELLY HOLMES

When a man starts
out to build a world,
he starts first with himself.

LANGSTON HUGHES

BE HEALTHY AND TAKE
CARE OF YOURSELF,
BUT BE HAPPY WITH
THE BEAUTIFUL
THINGS THAT
MAKE YOU, YOU.

Beyoncé

YOU CAN'T JUST SIT THERE AND WAIT FOR PEOPLE TO GIVE YOU THAT GOLDEN DREAM.

Diana Ross

If you look at how long the Earth has been here, we're living in the blink of an eye. So, whatever it is you want to do, you go out and do it.

Jamie Foxx

TAKE A STAND FOR WHAT'S RIGHT... YOU MAY NOT ALWAYS BE POPULAR, BUT YOU'LL BE PART OF SOMETHING LARGER AND BIGGER AND GREATER THAN YOURSELF. BESIDES, MAKING HISTORY IS EXTREMELY COOL.

SAMUEL L. JACKSON

WHATEVER IS BRINGING YOU DOWN, GET RID OF IT. BECAUSE YOU'LL FIND THAT WHEN YOU'RE FREE, YOUR TRUE CREATIVITY, YOUR TRUE SELF, COMES OUT.

Tina Turner

BEAUTY IS BEING
COMFORTABLE
AND CONFIDENT IN
YOUR OWN SKIN.

Iman

If you need help,
and someone is in a
position to help, you
should feel comfortable
to ask them.

MARCUS RASHFORD

YOU DON'T HAVE TO BE ANYTHING BUT YOURSELF TO BE WORTHY.

TARANA BURKE

"

I BELIEVE THAT IT IS
IMPORTANT TO NAME
THE MULTIPLE PARTS OF
MY IDENTITY BECAUSE I
AM NOT JUST ONE THING,
AND NEITHER ARE YOU.

Laverne Cox

BE PASSIONATE AND MOVE FORWARD WITH GUSTO EVERY SINGLE HOUR OF EVERY SINGLE DAY UNTIL YOU REACH YOUR GOAL.

AVA DuVERNAY

When you want
to succeed as
bad as you want
to breathe,
then you'll be
successful.

Eric Thomas

WE NEED TO BE

WILLING TO BE

UNCOMFORTABL

TO BE FLAWED,

TO BE IMPERFEC

TO OWN OUR

VOICE, TO STEP

INTO OUR LIGHT

I am not lucky. You know what I am? I am smart, I am talented, I take advantage of the opportunities that come my way... Don't call me lucky. Call me a badass.

SHONDA RHIMES

YOU ARE NEVER TOO OLD TO SET ANOTHER GOAL OR TO DREAM A NEW DREAM.

LES BROWN

EVERYBODY
ALWAYS HAS
SOMETHING
TO LEARN...
EVERYBODY
CAN ALWAYS
GET BETTER.

GAYLE KING

If you have a goal that is very, very far out, and you approach it in little steps, you start to get there faster.

MAE JEMISON

LIKE WHAT YOU DO,
AND THEN YOU WILL
DO YOUR BEST.

Katherine Johnson

BELIEVE,
DON'T FEAR,
BELIEVE.

Gabby Douglas

It isn't where
you came from,
it's where you're
going that counts.

Ella Fitzgerald

LIFE HAS MEANING ONLY IN THE STRUGGLE... SO LET US CELEBRATE THE STRUGGLE!

STEVIE WONDER

TO BE HUMAN IS TO
SEEK PERFECTION
AND FIND JOY IN
NEVER ATTAINING IT.

Lupita Nyong'o

IF YOU WANT TO FLY,
YOU HAVE TO GIVE
UP THE THINGS THAT
WEIGH YOU DOWN.

Toni Morrison

We should always be aspiring to know more, and to better ourselves, and to improve ourselves.

LAURYN HILL

THE PATH TO YOUR SUCCESS IS NOT AS FIXED AND INFLEXIBLE AS YOU THINK.

MISTY COPELAND

> **EVERYONE CAN RISE ABOVE THEIR CIRCUMSTANCES AND ACHIEVE SUCCESS IF THEY ARE DEDICATED TO AND PASSIONATE ABOUT WHAT THEY DO.**
>
> Nelson Mandela

If you're interested in finding out more about our books, find us on Facebook at **Summersdale Publishers** and follow us on Twitter at **@Summersdale**.

www.summersdale.com